THE *Vegetable* TRIVIA BOOK

By Jenine Zimmers

Copyright ©2023

HOW TO PLAY

Welcome to "The Vegetable Trivia Book,"
a collection of veggie trivia questions to
determine if you can truly call yourself a
plant-loving pro! Questions come in groups
of five, each pertaining to one specific
vegetable. You'll be tested on the origins of
various plants, classic vegetable dishes, and
even veggies in pop culture!

To play for points, divide into two teams.
Teams take turns tackling a vegetable
category, and answering all five questions
in it. One point is awarded for each correct
answer. Alternate reading and answering
questions for each category. You may play
the whole book in one game, or stop at
page 42 to play half. The team with the
most points at the end wins!

You may also test yourself by moving
through the book solo. As a bonus,
interesting veggie tidbits are sprinkled
throughout the pages for fun.

Enjoy!

CONTENTS

Artichokes

1. In what Asian country are artichokes used to make tea leaves?

2. True or false: Each artichoke plant produces about 50 artichokes.

3. What iconic actress was named Artichoke Queen in California in 1948?

4. The English word "artichoke" comes from the word "articiocco" in what language?

5. True or false: The Jerusalem artichoke is from Jerusalem.

ANSWERS

1. Vietnam

2. False. Each plant produces 15-20.

3. Marilyn Monroe

4. Italian

5. False. They grow in North America.

FUN FACT

An artichoke is technically
an unbloomed flower.

Asparagus

1. Which country grows the most asparagus in the world?

2. Green asparagus gets its color from exposure to what?

3. True or false: Green and white asparagus come from the same plant.

4. In what country can you find a museum dedicated to asparagus?

5. True or false: From seed, asparagus plants take 3 years to grow.

ANSWERS

ANSWERS

1 China

2 Sunlight

3 True!

4 Germany

5 True!

FUN FACT

Asparagus has been grown for thousands
of years, and was even depicted on
Egyptian tombs dating from 400 BC.

Beans

1. In Nicaragua, a bowl of beans is given to whom for good luck?

2. What U.S. state produces the most beans?

3. Mung Beans, the smallest bean, are native to what country?

4. Mexican jumping beans jump to escape what?

5. In the movie "Silence of the Lambs," Hannibal Lector ate what kind of beans?

1 Newlyweds

2 North Dakota

3 India

4 Sunlight

5 Fava beans

FUN FACT

There are more than 40,000 varieties of beans.

Beets

1. True or false: Beet leaves are edible.

2. What red soup is made from beets in Eastern Europe?

3. What well-known physicist hated beets?

4. In what country are pickled beets often put on hamburgers?

5. True or false: Larger beets are sweeter than smaller ones.

1. True!

2. Borscht

3. Albert Einstein

4. Australia or New Zealand

5. False. Smaller beets are sweeter.

FUN FACT

Early American colonists used beets
to create pink cake frosting.

Bell Peppers

1 Which has the most vitamin C,
a red, yellow, or green bell pepper?

2 True or false: Red bell peppers are
green bell peppers that have been
left on the vine to ripen.

3 China by far produces the most
bell peppers. What country
is second in production?

4 True or false: Bell peppers
can be purple.

5 What dried spice comes
from bell peppers?

1 Yellow pepper

2 True!

3 Mexico

4 True! Though they are rare.

5 Paprika

FUN FACT

"Pepperoni" is the Italian word for "bell pepper."
If you order a "pepperoni pizza" in Italy, you will
get bell peppers as a topping.

Broccoli

1. What is the term for the flowering stems that make up the head of broccoli?

2. What type of broccoli is known for its pyramid shape and many small spiral rosettes?

3. What U.S. president banned broccoli from being served on Air Force One?

4. In 1993, John Evans and Mary Evans grew the heaviest broccoli at 35 pounds in what U.S. state?

5. The word "broccoli" comes from the Italian plural of broccolo, which means "the flowering crest" of what other vegetable?

1 Florets

2 Romanesco

3 George H.W. Bush

4 Alaska

5 Cabbage

FUN FACT

When broccoli was first introduced in England in the mid-18th century, they called it "Italian asparagus."

Brussels Sprouts

1. What do Brussels sprouts contain that causes them to smell?

2. Brussels sprouts are named after the capital of what country?

3. True or false: Carving an X in the stem bottoms before steaming helps Brussels sprouts cook more evenly.

4. What cooking method actually enhances the cholesterol-lowering powers of fresh Brussels sprouts?

5. On what holiday are Brussels sprouts commonly served in Great Britain?

ANSWERS

1. Sulfur
2. Belgium
3. True!
4. Steaming
5. Christmas

FUN FACT

In 2013, a group of students and scientists in London powered the lights on a Christmas tree using energy from 1,000 Brussels sprouts.

Cabbage

1 What country consumes the most cabbage?

2 What legendary baseball player put cabbage in his baseball cap to stay cool?

3 Scrolls from 1000 BC found in China stated cabbage could be used to cure what for men?

4 What popular cabbage-themed doll debuted in 1983?

5 Irish immigrants popularized serving cabbage with what for St. Patrick's Day?

1. Russia
2. Babe Ruth
3. Baldness
4. Cabbage Patch Kid
5. Corned beef

FUN FACT

Cabbage is the main ingredient in sauerkraut.

Carrots

1. True or false: Cooked carrots are more nutritious than raw carrots.

2. In the 10th century, carrots were what color?

3. What cartoon character eats carrots?

4. What Middle Eastern country used carrots to make clothing dye for the rich and royal?

5. True or false: Eating too an excess of carrots can change your skin color.

1. True!

2. Purple

3. Bugs Bunny

4. Afghanistan

5. True!

FUN FACT

Holtville, California, calls itself the
"Carrot Capital of the World," and holds
an annual carrot festival.

Cauliflower

1 True or false: Cauliflower leaves are not edible.

---

2 In what year did cauliflower rice become an internet sensation: 2002, 2007, or 2012?

---

3 "Caulipower" pizza crust debuted in what grocery chain in 2017?

---

4 True or false: Cauliflower can be orange.

---

5 Broccoflower is the term sometimes used for what type of cauliflower?

1 False! They are edible.

2 2012

3 Whole Foods

4 True! It's sweeter than white.

5 Green

FUN FACT

Cauliflower contains some of almost every
vitamin and mineral that you need
for good health.

Celery

1. What well-known salad combines celery, fresh apples, walnuts, and grapes with mayonnaise dressing?

2. Celery is commonly used as a garnish in what tomato juice and vodka cocktail?

3. "Ants on a log" is a snack made using celery, peanut butter, and what?

4. Khloe Kardashian enjoys eating celery as a snack along with what nut?

5. True or false: In the 1960s, Jell-O offered celery-flavored gelatin mix.

1. Waldorf salad
2. Bloody Mary
3. Raisins
4. Almonds
5. True!

FUN FACT

The ancient Chinese used celery as medicine.

Chickpeas

1. Chickpeas are the main ingredient in what Middle Eastern dip?

2. What G word is another common name for chickpeas?

3. Chickpea powder has been used a substitute to make what morning beverage?

4. What country produces the most chickpeas?

5. Chickpeas can be used to treat what scalp condition?

1. Hummus
2. Garbanzo
3. Coffee
4. India
5. Dandruff

FUN FACT

The Ancient Romans believed that chickpeas were a gift from the Goddess Venus to help with fertility.

Collard Greens

1. Collard greens and what other dish are eaten for luck on New Year's Day in the southern U.S.?

2. Collard greens are the official state vegetable of what U.S. state?

3. Uncooked collard greens have what kind of flavor?

4. Which of the following is not a type of collard green: Ole Timey Blue, Morris Heading, Blue Moon, or Jade?

5. True or false: Collard greens cannot be served after being frozen.

1. Black-eyed peas
2. South Carolina
3. Bitter
4. Blue Moon
5. False! They freeze well.

FUN FACT

In Portugal and Brazil, collard greens are a common side dish to fish and meat.

Corn

1. What M word is another name
for corn?

2. According to Green Giant, corn
overtook what vegetable in 2023
as America's favorite?

3. What is the best season
to harvest and eat corn?

4. What 1984 horror film based on the
Stephen King short story contained
the word "corn" in the title?

5. What cereal brand invented
corn flakes?

1. Maize

2. Broccoli

3. Summer

4. "Children of the Corn"

5. Kellogg's

FUN FACT

An average ear of corn contains
about 800 kernels.

Eggplant

1 Americans call it an eggplant, but what do the Brits call it?

---

2 True or false: Eggplants contain nicotine.

---

3 What popular Lebanese dip is made using eggplant?

---

4 What U.S. state produces the most eggplants?

---

5 In what country is eggplant called brinjal and known as the "King of Vegetables"?

1 Aubergine

2 True! A very small amount.

3 Baba ganoush

4 New Jersey

5 India

FUN FACT

In the 1700s, early European versions of eggplant were smaller, and yellow or white. They looked like goose or chicken eggs, which led to the name "eggplant."

Green Beans

1. Green beans originally had a thin, fibrous seam that led to what common nickname for this vegetable?

2. A green bean pizza eating contest is held at the annual Green Bean Festival in what U.S. state?

3. What food company invented the green bean casserole?

4. Wax beans (or yellow beans) differ from green beans because they do not contain what?

5. Harvested young, green beans are actually an immature version of what bean?

1. Kidney bean
2. Georgia
3. Campbell's
4. Chlorophyll
5. String beans

FUN FACT

There are two types of green bean plants: pole beans, which grow like a climbing vine up to ten feet, and bush beans, which grow up to two feet.

Jalapeño Peppers

1. In what country did the jalapeño pepper originate?

2. What color is a fully ripe jalapeño pepper?

3. What type of cheese is commonly used in jalapeño poppers?

4. True or false: Removing seeds from a jalapeño pepper can make it less spicy.

5. If you smoke and dry a Jalapeño, what kind of pepper do you have?

ANSWERS

1. Mexico
2. Red
3. Cream cheese
4. True!
5. Chipotle

FUN FACT

Jalapeño peppers were taken on board the Columbia space shuttle in the 1980s and are the only chili pepper to have left Earth.

Kale

1. What U.S. state produces the most kale?

2. Scots kale is known for have what kind of leaves?

3. What is the process of briefly boiling kale called?

4. What fast food chain sued a T-shirt maker for using the phrase "Eat More Kale"?

5. What is the name of the pigment responsible for kale's green color?

1. California
2. Curly
3. Blanching
4. Chick-fil-A
5. Chlorophyll

FUN FACT

Kale becomes sweeter after a frost.

1. The leek is the national symbol of what country: England, Wales, or Ireland?

2. Vichyssoise is a classic French soup is made with leeks and what other vegetable?

3. True or false: The dark green part of a leek is edible.

4. Which country produces the most leeks: Indonesia, Turkey, or Belgium?

5. True or false: Leeks cannot survive extreme cold.

1. Wales

2. Potato

3. True! It is just a bit tougher.

4. Indonesia

5. False! They are very cold-tolerant.

FUN FACT

Leeks are toxic to dogs and cats,
so keep them away from your pets!

Lettuce

1. What explorer introduced lettuce to the United States?

2. What kind of lettuce is used in Caesar salad?

3. What H word is used to describe the innermost leaves in a head of lettuce?

4. What lettuce has a bitter taste and is often used in a mixed greens salad?

5. True or false: Lighter green lettuce is more nutritious.

1. Christopher Columbus

2. Romaine

3. Heart

4. Arugula

5. False: Darker green is more nutritious.

FUN FACT

On average, each American eats 30 pounds of lettuce every year.

Mushrooms

1. What is the term for the above-ground, umbrella-like part of a mushroom?

2. Which video game is mainly set in a place called the Mushroom Kingdom?

3. Which mushroom is more rare, black truffles or white truffles?

4. What type of mushroom shares its name with a musical instrument?

5. What is the most popular mushroom in Japanese cooking?

1. Cap
2. Super Mario Bros.
3. White truffles
4. Trumpet
5. Shiitake

FUN FACT

Mushrooms are neither plants nor animals. They constitute their own kingdom: Fungi.

1. What Louisiana stew commonly features okra?

2. Some people don't like that okra can feel what way after being cooked?

3. In what U.S. state can you find Delta State University, home of the Fighting Okra?

4. Soldiers used ground okra as a coffee substitute during what American War?

5. What famous chef known for New Orleans cuisine prepares several dishes featuring okra?

1. Gumbo
2. Slimy (or gummy)
3. Mississippi
4. Civil War
5. Emeril Lagasse

FUN FACT

Okra is known as "lady fingers"
in some parts of the world.

Onions

1. True or false: Before it was known as "The Big Apple," New York City was called "The Big Onion."

2. What type of cheese is traditionally used in French onion soup?

3. The Walla Walla Sweet Onion is the official vegetable of what U.S. state: Washington, Wyoming, or Virginia?

4. Green onions are also known by what other name?

5. What herb can you eat to eliminate onion breath?

1. True!

2. Gruyère (or Swiss)

3. Washington

4. Scallions

5. Parsley (or mint)

FUN FACT

During the ancient Olympic games in Greece, athletes prepared by drinking onion juice and rubbing onions on their bodies to warm muscles.

Parsnips

1. What type of vegetable is a parsnip?

2. Parsnips were the main form of dietary starch in the United States until what vegetable became popular?

3. True or false: The paler the parsnip, the sweeter it is.

4. In Europe, parsnips were used to sweeten jams and cakes before what was widely available?

5. True or false: Parsnips are a good source of vitamin C.

1. Root vegetable
2. Potato
3. True!
4. Sugar
5. False. They contain very little.

FUN FACT

During Roman times, Emperor Tiberius accepted parsnips as part of a tribute from the people of what is now known as Germany.

1. What popular fairy tale by Hans Christian Andersen contains the word pea in the title?

2. Ärtsoppa is a pea soup popular in what country: Denmark, Sweden, or Norway?

3. Green peas contain more of this per serving than any other vegetable.

4. What food brand was the first to offer frozen peas?

5. In 1984, Janet Harris broke a Guinness World Record by eating 7,175 peas using what utensil?

1. "The Princess and the Pea"
2. Sweden
3. Protein
4. Birdseye
5. Chopsticks

FUN FACT

The proper etiquette for eating peas is to squash them on the back of your fork.

Potatoes

1. What fast food chain added the baked potato to its menu in 1983?

---

2. What food company began making "Tator Tots" in 1954?

---

3. Which U.S. vice president is remembered for incorrectly spelling "potato" in an elementary classroom?

---

4. What U.S. state has a museum dedicated to potatoes?

---

5. What potato-themed toy was the first ever toy to be advertised on television?

ANSWERS

1. Wendy's
2. Ore-Ida
3. Dan Quayle
4. Idaho
5. Mr. Potato Head

FUN FACT

Potatoes are said to "grow eyes"
as they age.

Pumpkins

1. What color are pumpkins before they turn orange?

2. In what year did Starbucks start selling the Pumpkin Spice Latte: 2003, 2005, or 2007?

3. Legend says that pumpkin can remove what from your face?

4. Who wrote the book "Waiting For The Great Pumpkin"?

5. True or false: Pumpkin pie was served at the first Thanksgiving.

1 Green

2 2003

3 Freckles

4 Charles M. Schulz

5 False. There is no evidence a pumpkin pie was served.

FUN FACT

The word pumpkin came from the Greek word "pepon" which means "large melon."

Radishes

1. What country holds an annual festival where contestants carve and sculpt art from radishes?

2. True or false: Radish leaves are edible.

3. Ancient Egyptians used radish oil before what oil was discovered?

4. What kind of radish is known for long, white roots and mild flavor?

5. What type of radish has a bright pink interior?

1. Mexico
2. True!
3. Olive oil
4. Daikon radish
5. Watermelon radish

FUN FACT

Radishes, onions and garlic were paid as wages to the Ancient Egyptian laborers who built the Pyramids.

Rhubarb

1. In the United States, June 9 is a national day celebrating rhubarb pie made with what fruit?

2. True or false: The leaves attached to a Rhubarb stalk are poisonous.

3. In 1947, rhubarb was legally classified as this in the United States.

4. A baseball broadcaster popularized the word rhubarb as slang for what in the 1930s?

5. True or false: Rhubarb contains absolutely no fiber.

ANSWERS

1. Strawberry

2. True!

3. Fruit. But is a vegetable!

4. A fight

5. False! It is high in fiber.

FUN FACT

Benjamin Franklin's cure for flatulence was dried rhubarb and attar of roses dissolved in wine.

Spinach

1. What cartoon character loved eating Spinach?

2. True or false: Spinach was the first frozen vegetable available in grocery stores.

3. What magazine ran a cartoon of a child turning down spinach in 1928 that led to kids hating the vegetable?

4. What country is known for spanakopita, a savory spinach pie?

5. In medieval times, people extracted green pigment from spinach to use as what?

1. Popeye
2. True!
3. The New Yorker
4. Greece
5. Ink, or paint

FUN FACT

Popeye's popularity increased consumption of spinach in the United States by 33 percent in the 1930s, which was much needed during the Great Depression.

Squash

1. True or false: Whole butternut squash can last up to a month once in your kitchen.

2. What type of squash has a dark green skin and a sweet, nutty flavor?

3. Red kuri squash is native to what country: India, Japan, or Vietnam?

4. Which stays on the vine longer, summer squash or winter squash?

5. True or false: Zucchini is a type of squash.

1 True!

2 Acorn squash

3 Japan

4 Winter squash

5 True!

FUN FACT

Squashes are commonly made into candies
in Latin America.

Tomatoes

1. What 1991 movie starring Kathy Bates and Jessica Tandy had tomatoes in the title?

2. Caprese salad is an Italian salad featuring tomatoes and what cheese?

3. What company sold the first bottle of tomato ketchup in 1876?

4. In what country does La Tomatina, a festival and tomato-based food fight, take place?

5. What American website that reviews film and TV shows has tomatoes as part of its name?

1. "Fried Green Tomatoes"

2. Mozzarella

3. Heinz

4. Spain

5. Rotten Tomatoes

FUN FACT

Tomatoes are a fruit, but legally considered a vegetable in the United States.

Turnips

1. Original jack-o-lanterns were made using turnips instead of pumpkins in what country?

2. True or false: The turnip's closest vegetable relative is a potato.

3. What playwright used turnips as an insult?

4. The top of most turnip bulbs are what color?

5. What country has a dish called "Neeps and Tatties," which means turnips and potatoes: Scotland, Ireland, or Wales?

1 Ireland

2 False. It's radish and arugula.

3 William Shakespeare

4 Purple

5 Scotland

FUN FACT

The smaller the bulb of a turnip,
the sweeter it will taste.

Yams

1. True or false: Yams are another name for sweet potatoes.

2. The large majority of the world's yams are grown on what continent?

3. True or false: Certain types of yams cannot be eaten raw.

4. Candied yams were actually invented as a way for a food company to sell more of what?

5. Cinnamon vine is another name for what type of yam: Japanese, Chinese, or Taiwanese?

ANSWERS

1. False. They are different vegetables
2. Africa
3. True!
4. Marshmallows
5. Chinese yam

FUN FACT

In some West African languages,
the word "yam" means "to eat."

Zucchini

1 In what country were 10,000-year-old zucchini seeds found in caves: Honduras, Chile, or Mexico?

2 Zucchini means "little squash" in what language?

3 What is the name for zucchini in France, Great Britain and New Zealand?

4 What color is the flower of zucchini?

5 True or false: One zucchini is a "zucchina."

ANSWERS

1. Mexico
2. Italian
3. Courgette
4. Yellow
5. True!

FUN FACT

A zucchini has more potassium
than a banana.

Thank you!

The purchase of this book supported
a small business. We hope you enjoyed it!

www.ingramcontent.com/pod-product-compliance
Lightning Source LLC
Chambersburg PA
CBHW060758260726
48660CB00002B/685